creature comforts

A Brazilian jaguar, lounging disconsolately in his cage at the zoo, shrugs helplessly. 'We need the space to live,' he moans, 'We need the space to feel we are part of the world...'

To Andrew.
Happy Christmas.

[signature]

C00014359

The jaguar — along with his zoo companions — has become an international celebrity after appearing in CREATURE COMFORTS, Nick Park's Oscar-winning film for Aardman Animations.

The creatures were brought to life in a former warehouse in Bristol that is a cross between a studio and a kid's playroom. There are lights, cameras, videos and more Plasticine (in the most fabulous colours) than any child ever imagined in its wildest dreams!

For the remarkable thing about the CREATURE COMFORTS characters is that they are all made of Plasticine — as was Morph, Tony Hart's mischievous companion on BBC children's television, the earliest creation of Peter Lord and David Sproxton who founded Aardman Animations.

At Work on CREATURE COMFORTS.

Then came CONVERSATION PIECES, a series of adult films for Channel 4 about human communication (and the lack of it!) using a documentary-style sound-track recorded with 'fly-on-the-wall' methods. The Plasticine actors were brought to life in what is known as 'stop-frame' animation, a technique which requires the models to be moved very slightly for each frame of film. With twenty-four frames for every second of film, this is a slow, painstaking process.

CREATURE COMFORTS began with the idea of asking what people thought about zoos. The answers were almost all the same — zoos were basically a good idea, but conditions could be better. So to make it more interesting they added an inspired twist by asking people in hostels and old people's homes how they felt about where they lived. Hence the bush-baby who (despite having a creaking tree) feels 'very secure' and a bored turtle who 'escapes into books and things'.

Nick Park's genius as an animator is his ability to give gestures and expressions to his animals — the turtle's nervous swallow, the jaguar's frustrated frown, the father polar bear's embarrassed grin — that make us laugh because they are so very human.

'Animals in the zoo,' says one of the funny blue birds, 'can do their own thing....' Certainly that's true of the animals in Aardman's zoo.

Brian Sibley

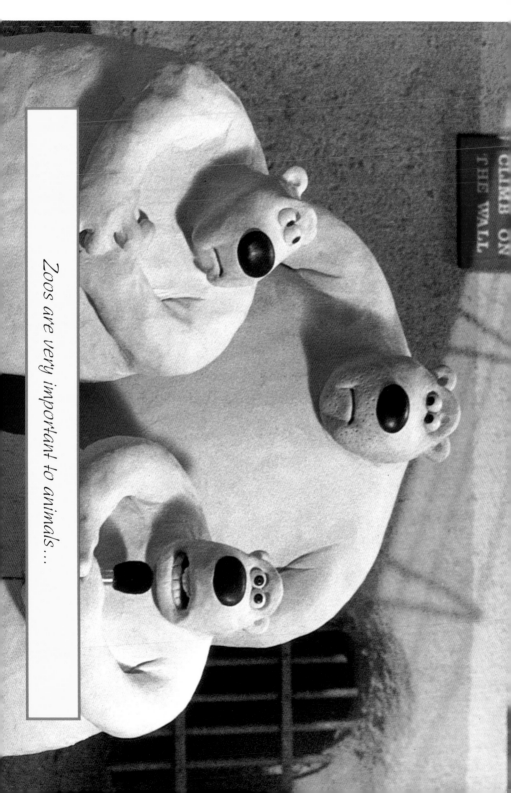

Zoos are very important to animals ...

AARD.....MAN   AN....   I...   MA.....TIONS

Zoos are a bit like nursing homes for poor animals.

AARD......MAN   AN...   I....   M.....   ...TIONS

From CREATURE COMFORTS AT LARGE.
published by Macdonald and based on
CREATURE COMFORTS. commissioned by
Channel Four Television. produced by Aardman
Animations Ltd. © Aardman Animations Ltd 1989.

People in the wild don't have much to eat so they have to kill their own people...

AARD... ...MAN   AN... I...   MA... ...TIONS

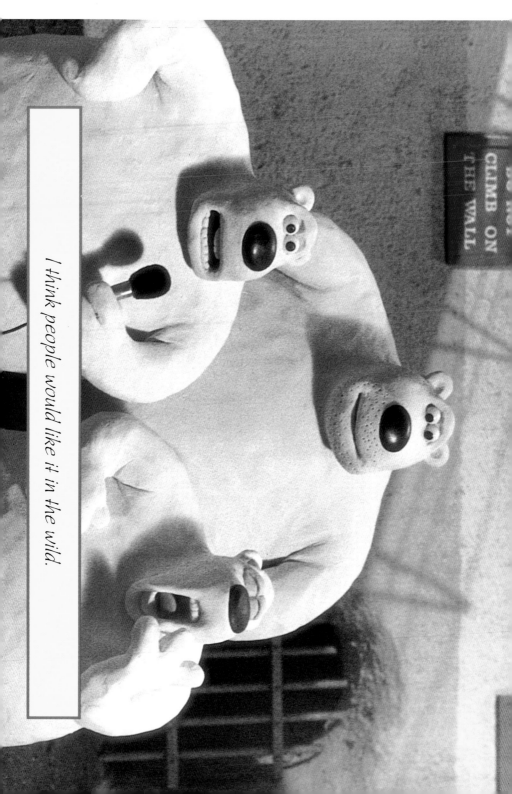

I think people would like it in the wild.

From CREATURE COMFORTS AT LARGE,
published by Macdonald and based on
CREATURE COMFORTS, commissioned by
Channel Four Television, produced by Aardman
Animations Ltd. © Aardman Animations Ltd 1989.

PLACE
STAMP
HERE

My favourite food, I'm afraid to say, is steak.

AARD....MAN   AN...   I...   MA.....TIONS

Do you like lions? Do you like steak and chips with lions with it?

AARD.....MAN   AN...   I...   MA.....TIONS

From CREATURE COMFORTS AT LARGE.
published by Macdonald and based on
CREATURE COMFORTS, commissioned by
Channel Four Television, produced by Aardman
Animations Ltd. © Aardman Animations Ltd 1989.

It's very, very good here, very comfortable you know ...

AARD....MAN   AN.... I... MA.... ...TIONS

We're well looked after and it's in a nice position.

AARD....MAN   AN...   L....   M.A......TIONS

Most of the cages are a bit small...

AARD.....MAN   AN.... I... MA.... .TIONS

From CREATURE COMFORTS AT LARGE,
published by Macdonald and based on
CREATURE COMFORTS, commissioned by
Channel Four Television, produced by Aardman
Animations Ltd. © Aardman Animations Ltd 1989.

It's, er, like grotty and everything.

AARD....MAN   AN... I... MA... ..TIONS

My room is a bit too small really, and I've got <u>so much</u> stuff in it.

AARD.....MAN   AN.....I.....   MA.....TIONS

I've been in more comfortable rooms …

AARD....MAN AN.....I... MA.......TIONS

I try to spend as little time as possible in here...

From CREATURE COMFORTS AT LARGE,
published by Macdonald and based on
CREATURE COMFORTS, commissioned by
Channel Four Television, produced by Aardman
Animations Ltd. © Aardman Animations Ltd 1989.

If I can't get out and about, I sort of escape into books and things…

AARD....MAN   AN....   I....   MA.... ..TIONS

I feel very secure and well looked after…

AARD.....MAN   AN..... I... MA.....TIONS

From CREATURE COMFORTS AT LARGE,
published by Macdonald and based on
CREATURE COMFORTS, commissioned by
Channel Four Television, produced by Aardman
Animations Ltd. © Aardman Animations Ltd 1989.

I'm not worried about anything.

AARD......MAN AN.... I... MA.... ...TIONS

I know that whatever happens, they'll look after me and put me where I ought to be...

AARD....MAN   AN...   I....   MA.....TIONS

From CREATURE COMFORTS AT LARGE.
published by Macdonald and based on
CREATURE COMFORTS, commissioned by
Channel Four Television, produced by Aardman
Animations Ltd. © Aardman Animations Ltd 1989.

Animals in the circus have to get up on boxes and balls.

PLACE
STAMP
HERE

Animals in the zoo don't have to do anything.

PLACE
STAMP
HERE

Here you can do your own thing.

Sometimes I can't get out and about as much as I'd like to.

AARD... ...MAN   AN...   I...   MA...   ...TIONS

I'm often stuck inside for some reason, like I'm stuck in today.

AARD... ...MAN AN... I... MA... ...TIONS

I get bored and fed up looking at the same four walls every day.

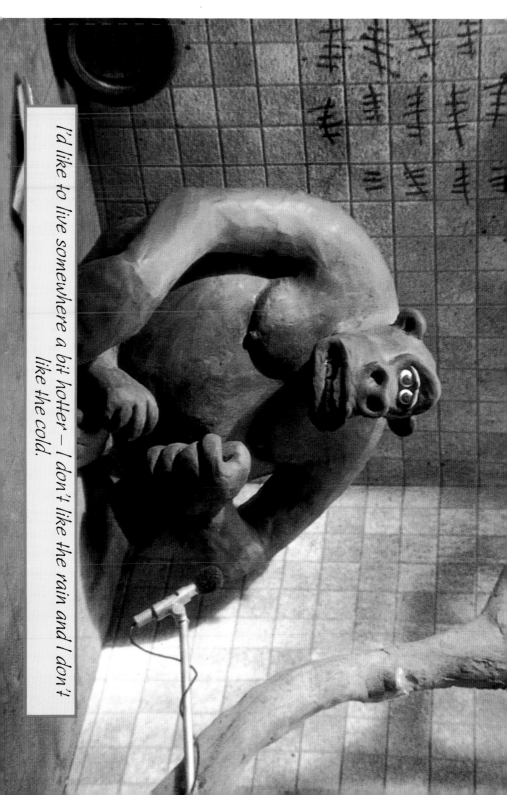

I'd like to live somewhere a bit hotter — I don't like the rain and I don't like the cold.

In Brazil, you have <u>space</u> …

From CREATURE COMFORTS AT LARGE,
published by Macdonald and based on
CREATURE COMFORTS, commissioned by
Channel Four Television, produced by Aardman
Animations Ltd. © Aardman Animations Ltd 1989.

In the zoo, you live in a very small place.

AARD....MAN AN.... I.... MA.... ...TIONS

We need _space_ to feel that we are part of the world and not just a piece of an object in a box.

From CREATURE COMFORTS AT LARGE.
published by Macdonald and based on
CREATURE COMFORTS. commissioned by
Channel Four Television. produced by Aardman
Animations Ltd. © Aardman Animations Ltd 1989.

I'd like to live in a hot country with good weather.

PLACE
STAMP
HERE

I'd like to have nice weather with blue skies so that I can see the sun every day...

AARD....MAN   AN....   I....   MA....   ...TIONS